Encouraging Words to Lift your Spirit Up Now

By

Donald Coad

ISBN: 0-75965-005-5

This book is printed on acid free paper.

1stBooks - rev. 08/01/01

Safe in Your Arms

Safe in your arms no one can do me any harm.
Dwelling in your house, giving you the praise.
My faith in your promise your word shall never fade away.
All of my trust I put in you.
I can't depend on anyone else, this is why I call on you.
Some things in life we question why.
But nevertheless, your will be done and not mine.
Thank you Jesus – my tongue is not enough to say I love you, Lord;
even when I did not give you the praise.
Lord, you are so good, I don't know why.
Perhaps it is your Holy Spirit that is so kind.
Why does the world run away from thee?
You have the keys to the tree of life and the book of our eternity.
Safe in your arms, Jesus, that's where I want to be.

Safe in your arms when I'm riding through the storm.
Safe in your arms, nothing can do me any harm.

It's Me

It's Me, it's Me that gives you the ability when you wonder if you can't.
In other words, you should know me as Moses did.
Jehovah GOD – I am that I am.
It's Me, it's Me that gives you hope for a brighter day.
It's Me, it's Me I am the one who can make your life focus on my Son.
He is in Me, and I am in thee.
But just remember whatever you do, it's Me, it's Me.
Whatever you say, I have the power over the Prince of this world today.
It's me, not you – I've paid the price for I am the one who gave his life.
Because I love you and you're so dear, I'll keep you from all dangers far and near.
It's me, it's Me – I will always be.
I am the beginning and the end – I promise, you'll see.

No matter what life brings you – the highs or the lows,
Just always remember who is in control.
I am your Savior, your Rock and Shield – protecting you everyday.
So don't ever think that it's you – you'll only mess up and get in my way.
It's Me, it's Me – have a blessed and peaceful day!

Don't Look Back

If you don't look back you will be able to succeed.
 If you don't look back you'll gain the victory.
Listen to this story about a man named Jack.
 He was a successful businessman who thought that he became successful on his own.
However, God saw Jack through, despite his bad attitude.
 Jack became so large that he thought that he was God.
You see, Jack started to smoke crack.
 His wife and children noticed how he started to slack.
He slacked in his duties as a man; Satan took him by the hand.
 The problem with Jack was that he needed the Lord,
and Satan wasn't about to let him go.
 Jack was so out of whack from smoking crack, the Devil gave him a name

to announce to everyone that he was in the game.

"Cracker Jack," Satan called him, and death would be his prize.

But Jesus was praying for Jack, telling him to arise.

Jesus had to visit Jack in a special way.

He cleansed him from all unrighteousness and started Jack on his way.

Hey, don't look back, Jack, for all along it was the Devil's crack that had your mind.

I've come to you this day to tell you that you are all mine.

Man

My friend, you have tried everything and it has failed.
  Put your trust in Jesus – to the cross your sins were nailed.
Man will fail you every time.
  It's because he doesn't understand the power of the divine.
Man thinks he has created and done all these great things.
  If it were not for Jesus, man could not do anything.
Who gave man the power to think, walk and climb?
  It is God Almighty, the Maker of time.
Man can only get what God allows him to have.
  God can take it all from him and really make man sad.
Man can't cause the Sun to shine, nor can he stop God's rain.
  Man can only hope that God doesn't allow him to suffer much pain.

Man needs to stop and pray, thanking God in a blessed way
for giving man ideas that help in life each and everyday.
A hope for the future that the world would be saved.

Follow Me

If you follow me, I'll promise you eternity.
Drop all your cares, pick up your cross and I'll be there.
In times of trouble, just call on my name.
I'll be there in a hurry – trouble won't last always.
If you decide to follow me and go where I go, there are few things that I would like for you to know.
Some people will think you've lost your mind.
Even those in your family might say, "you can't be one of our kind."
Listen, I'll teach you how to be a good leader also.
For one day, someone will follow you, too.
To be a good follower, you must first have a good leader.
So follow Christ – his teachings in leadership are always right.
Following Jesus has made me strong.
Before Jesus came into my life,

I would follow people who didn't want to do right.

Now, I can truly say

I can't let a day go by without the Lord showing me the way.

The Most High God

Most High God – ruler of creation.
Holy one of Israel – Holy one of this nation.
Prince of Peace – Bright Morning Star.
Hope for tomorrow-that's who you are.
Wonderful Counselor – guiding light
who gives me the strength to stand and fight.
There is a war going on and it is plain to see
how the battle is affecting you and also affecting me.
But, with a made up mind and a soldier's attitude
with Christ on our side, he will see us through.
God is always there – sometimes it is hard for us to see.
That's just a trick of satan's – Saints of God, we have the victory.
Keep your focus on the King, singing praises to God.
Let joy bells ring – ring out loud in the land.
So pleasing to God – sounding so grand.

Great is the Lord

Great is the Lord of our salvation.
Come into our hearts and fulfill your destination.
In my life I turn over to you the things I cannot bear.
Your power in handling these matters is the reason I cast my cares.
Be glorified in everything, let your will be done.
This I know deep within my heart, you are the chosen one.
Life without you would be very hard.
To live without you, my life would be complete sin.
But when God looks at Jesus, my sin is no longer sin.
I bless you O' Lord at all times.
For the blessing of Jesus is pure and one of a kind.
The love that you shared at Calvary –
no one could ever share such love for someone like me.

This is why I always say – Great is the Lord and Greatly to be praised.

Come Out of the Darkness

Come out of the darkness and into the light.
Jesus is calling you to do things right.
I know all your feelings, you don't think there's anything wrong.
You think you got it all together, you think you got it going on.
The house is nice, the car is fine.
The job you have, it's one of a kind.
The money you make and blow makes my mind wonder how you can live this way.
God has blessed you with so much and you don't give God the time of day.
Remember how your Mom and Dad used to bring you to church.
How they prayed to God that he would give you the most.
Their prayers were answered – God did what they asked.
But as you grew older, you turned your back.

You went into darkness pondering on material things.
The devil was using you, waiting to take you under his wing.
He filled your mind with darkness to make things seem right.
While all along, the Holy Spirit was calling–
Saying, "come out of the darkness and step into the light."

Do You have to Go?

I asked the question, "Do you have to go?"
My heart and mind wanted the answer to be "No."
You explained the importance of your departing and now I want the world to know
why I asked the question, "Do you have to go?"
I pondered when you told me the reasons why.
Why you had to go to Calvary's cross to be crucified and die.
My heart was so heavy that my soul started to cry.
Then you whispered softly, "on the third day I will arise."
You said, "If I don't go, the Comforter will not come.
If I don't go, the world won't believe that I am the true Son.
The true Son of God filled with the Holy Ghost.
You'll no longer see me, but I'll be on my post.

Yes, I have to go so that men and women will know
that Jesus the Christ conquered death and made the devil an open show."

Worship the Lord in Spirit and Truth

When we worship the Lord we worship him in spirit and truth.
For our God is an awesome God – do I have to give you proof?
I will give you proof for it is in his word.
Lift up the Savior for men to see.
He promised in his word I will draw all men unto Me.
As we worship God we will be in the presence of holiness at the Master's feet.
Worship the Lord in spirit and truth and your troubled mind will become clear.
Those that say they love Jesus won't have any fears.
So keep your mind on Jesus and the devil will flee.
If you're having trouble doing this just ask a prayer warrior, "can you pray with me?"
Worship the Lord in spirit and truth.
The Bible tells us to do these things and that's all my proof.

The Bishop

Bishop Brown-it was destined to be.
How could it not, your father named you junior for the world to see.
I see him in you and you in him.
I see the love of Jesus and the souls that you win.
A soul winner – that's what you are
and on the darkest of nights you're a shining star.
Reign in your position – reign as a king.
Be loyal to your subjects and you'll receive greater things.
Thank you for your example – thank you for all you do.
Thank you for pastoring us – it helps us get through.

Don't You Worry, Heber

Don't you worry, just behold.
I have ordered your steps and I am in control.
Be not weary in your well doing.
The promise I have given you just keep pursuing.
Be not afraid when you don't see the flock.
I am in the midst of everything – at the door I stand and knock.
Don't let others hold you back.
I have blessed you with many gifts to share with those who lack.
When the Shiloh Church is overflowing, and I shall do it within this year,
I promised I would take care of you, Heber – you are so dear.
Preach on in my name;
the victory will be our gain.
What seems to be a problem now
I will remove it and this is my vow.

Going With His Flow

Lord, you know how I feel.
With your anointing, your presence is real.
I am going with His flow.
Jesus Christ's, don't you know.
Basically, when we are on one accord
the anointing of God is a two-edged sword.
It will cut the devil up – he won't have a chance
to enter your mind, you'll be able to dance.
Going with his flow, it can't be wrong.
Seeing all of his blessings I am singing a new song.
When I flow with him, it causes me to hate sin.
I love to worship and be in the flow,
also being in the cloud of the after glow.
Holy Spirit, teach us the way to flow
so the body of Christ can spiritually grow.
Going with this flow will bring us closer to the King.
Behold Shiloh, I will do a new thing.

Hold on Until the End

Hold on until the end.
You can make it, God still forgives your sins.
You think that you're too far gone.
Satan keeps telling you that your life is nothing so you can't go on.
I've come to tell you to hold on until the end for the promises of God are true.
The devil is a liar from the beginning to the end.
He never speaks the truth – he wants you to sin.
Our God is faithful – always trust in him; his son Jesus is on our side.
With his stripes we are healed.
With his spirit we are sealed.
There is no problem too big or too small.
Our God is able to catch us when we are about to fall.
Hold on until the end – it will make you strong.
It's not to discourage you, but to make you go on.

The devil keeps trying to hold you back,
bringing up failures of your past.
Hold on to the end, don't think you are nothing at all.
Hold on to Jesus, he has given us a new song.
A song of faith, a song of joy divine.
A song of victory to know Jesus is mine.

I Really Need You Now

I really need you now – my life is full of pain.
Yesterday my feelings were hurt and everyone said I was the blame.
I really need you now – I shouldn't have made you wait.
Please forgive me Jesus – I hope it's not too late.
I've done so many bad things in life-is it still possible for me to enter into your gates?
I really need you now because I don't know where to go.
My heart is really searching for the rivers of life that make me flow.
Flow to a new life – one that doesn't have envy or strife,
one that can make me understand.
I need you to take control of my life and I'll follow your commands.
I really need you now, and you've been with me all the time.
My faith in you has shown me that I really need you now.

Anyone can change – but Jesus will remain the same.
He has changed me for the best
and I'm sure he's not finished with me yet.
No more pain, no more blame.
I'm with Jesus now and that is my gain.

Be Aware

Be aware of the devil's snares.
He will trick you if you are unaware.
Presenting your sin before God, accusing the saints with any type of charge
so that our testimonies would be flawed.
When you serve the true, Living God, satan tries to make life awfully hard.
Don't give up – stay the course; Jesus will make a way.
He'll turn your sorrows into dancing – it will soon feel like a new day.
Be aware of satan's devices, he will use anyone to spoil our Christian walk in the light.
I found out something in these times of tests.
Holding on to Jesus is what I do best.
Because when I am weak, he is strong.
When I cling to Jesus, he won't prolong.
So in all of your efforts be aware when satan comes to buffet you.
Cast all of your cares – cast them onto Jesus, Master of everything.

Conquering satan once and for all, for all of his accusing future and past.

If you feel down and don't think you can finish the God-given task

remember this, the first shall be last and the last shall be first.

If you study your Bible, this should give you hope.

So be aware satan, the Children of God will shout,

"Victory is ours," because of your sin.

The tricks are over, your sin is condemned.

It's over now, the Saints of God win.

Hold Your Peace

Satan, you're not that smart.
If I keep my peace, I'll stop what you tried to start.
The confusion that you wanted to see
I can guarantee, on this day, you won't see it from me.
When confusion and chaos enters into your day
stop before you react – the Holy Spirit will teach you how to talk in a Godly way.
The devil thought he had me, but I got away.
The Holy Spirit spoke to me and gave me peace today.
I know satan tries to trick us anyway that he can.
He brings up the pettiest situations to get us to sin.
But remember Daniel and his peace when he was thrown in the lion's den.
So the next time when trouble takes you by surprise
know that Christ lives inside.
God is not pleased when we lose control.

He only looks for us to show his love for others to behold.

Any Blood Won't Do

Any blood won't do, it has to be a type of blood that can identify with you.
The blood of goats or the blood of rams won't be able to withstand.
This blood has to have power when it is shed
to let the world know the crucified one will not remain dead.
It's the blood of Jesus – I'll let everyone know
when they crucify my Son, his precious blood will flow.
The blood that cleanses sin from day to day.
I'll give it such power that you can plead the blood of Jesus when Satan tries to get in your way.
Any other type of blood won't be accepted – it could never pay the cost
because God has given us his son Jesus, the blood that saves the lost.

I Shall Never Die

I shall never die-even when you try to kill me with your words
or try to stop me from living in the 'burbs.
I shall never die-that will always be my plea.
Therefore, I will always think about my destiny.
I will arise in the morning giving God the praise.
Thanking Him for His blessing, for the dawn of a new day.
I shall never die-for he paid the price for me
with the death of Jesus on the cross at Calvary.
I shall never die-I will never quit because of my ancestors' courage and strength.
I shall never die after seeing and hearing about their struggles.
I will not be denied for they've paved a road for me;
a road to victory for our children's children to see.

I now reap the benefits, getting blessings that I have not sown.
    Because of these benefits, my people now own their own homes.
I shall never die – Christ gave his life to save the world you see.
    To give us an example of what the word struggle really means.
So don't give up – don't you die;
    Fight on, fight on – ye shall never die.

Shiloh of Edgemere

The people are coming from everywhere.
Not concerned about the distance for they know there's a blessing in store for them there.
A place of healing in times like these.
A place of comfort to meet your every need.
I've been to many churches, but this one is one of a kind.
Shiloh, you have welcomed my family with love divine.
Pastor Brown preaches with love, power and unity.
Three elements of God that we, as the body of Christ, need.
The people are a blessing and it does show.
Why there's even a couple that travels from Virginia – that' something to behold.
This town is in for a change as God continues to bring people from near and far.
Some give others a ride – those that don't have a car.
The church is able to soar
and the devil is running out the door.

Praising God for the great things He has done.

Not being selfish because God gave us his only begotten Son.

Hope

When you have hope, you have me.
When you have hope, it is hard not to see.
Hope is what gets me through the day.
Hope is a promise – can you show my people the way?
I can give you hope for a generation lost on dope.
I can meet your needs – you don't have to smoke weed.
I can pay your bills – you don't have to go out to steal and kill.
I can show you the way things can get better for you this day.
Hope will give you patience for all the world to see.
Hope will let you trust in Jesus – he will give you the victory.
When things in life seem to get you down, hope in Christ – he is in your town.
Don't give up – fight the good fight of faith.

Life is full of challenges and hope will show us the way.
Have faith for your future – that is all I have to say.

You Can Do All

You can speak peace to me and it will be so.
You can call my name and I will go.
You can give a word on high.
You can do anything, so why can't I.
You can make the sun shine through a cloudy haze.
You can make the birds sing on our darkest days.
You can make the sky so bright when we have the blues.
You can do whatever you want, I will still follow you.
You feed the hungry when they need to be fed.
You can shelter those who need a roof over their heads.
You can give your power to anyone you choose.
You can do whatever you wish, we have nothing to lose.

The Tithe

The tithe is a blessing for you and for me.
But you say how can that be?
God gave his Son so we could live.
In other words, God was showing us how to give.
The tithe is sacred – don't be misled.
The tithe is what kept the widows and less fortunate fed.
God wants us to tithe only ten percent.
A small portion of the many blessings that have been sent.
So trust and obey – have some faith today.
Prove God and see what great joy it will bring unto thee.
What if God asked you why?
Why didn't you honor me with the giving of the tithe?
What will you say or what will you do?
How will you answer God when he asks this question of you?
You robbed me so much the Holy Spirit is grieved.
Don't listen to satan, stop being deceived.

Follow my commandments and you will see. I'll pour you out a blessing you will not have room enough to receive.

I Did it for You

Sit down and listen to what I have to say.
It will not take long – I'll be short on this subject today.
I left Heaven's splendor to be crucified.
I did it for you – this is why I died.
I came to earth, grew from baby to man.
I did it for you that you might stand.
I healed many infirmities.
I did it for you and not for me.
I taught about love for your fellow brother.
I did it for you to share with each other.
I fed you when you had nothing to eat.
I did it for you that my spirit you might seek.
Finally, I can tell you why I died.
So the God of the heavens would be glorified
and I did it for you so you could not be denied.

Have You Ever Heard About Jesus

I would like to ask you a question because I'm wondering why.

Have you ever heard about Jesus?

Have you ever heard about the Word and how it was sent?

How God planned it and Jesus went?

He left Heaven's splendor to come to the earth.

To teach us about his Father's goodness and the lives he re-birthed.

Jesus came to give us the most.

We can't do anything without him, so don't even boast.

He can change your lifestyle if you give him a chance.

Just like the man in the tombs when people saw him they didn't just glance.

They heard he had been in the presence of Jesus – won't you let him in?

Have you ever heard about Jesus, how he calmed the sea?

How he rebuked Peter and also the Pharisees?

Have you ever heard about Jesus and the woman at the well?

After their conversation, she had a story to tell.
A Roman soldier had heard and asked Jesus to just send the word.
Jesus saw this man had faith – these kinds of things make living for Jesus great!

I Will Give You Rest After the Test

In this life there will be many tests.
After you've finished them, I will give you rest.
Every battle that you face I want you to continue at a slow pace.
A pace so you can go on, even when you're going through a storm.
God has your life in his hand – the test is not to cause you stress.
It's to assure you of a heavenly rest.
The days are long and the nights are quick.
Don't try to fight on your own – this fight is already fixed.
Keep the faith in God and be of good cheer.
Don't doubt what God is doing – he hasn't given us a spirit of fear.
So just remember this – I will give you rest after the test.

Heaven or Hell

I have a story to tell.
It's about Heaven and Hell.
Heaven is a place where I want you to go.
Heaven is a place to rest your weary soul.
Heaven is the home of our God and soon coming King.
Heaven is the place for you and the place for me.
Heaven is what I've been hearing about on this journey called life.
If it's anything like the preacher claims it to be,
then Heaven is the home I want in my final destiny.
To be with my Savior Jesus and live eternally.
Let me just say I have more words on the way about a place called Hell.
A place prepared for Lucifer and fallen angels who backslid and fell.
Hell is a place that grows from day to day,
Waiting for your loved ones who Jesus wants to save.

Hell is a dying place – rotten and decayed.
Waiting for your soul to come so you can be in pain.
Hell is not something that you see on T.V.
Hell is a place created for those who continue to do evil – it's a reality.

We Will Survive

I know you think that we will fall.
But I'm here to let you know that with Jesus on our side we will stand tall.
We will survive through the storms and the rain.
Even through the sadness and the pain.
Sometimes up, sometimes down,
but always remember that our Savior is always around
to get you through the toughest of times.
Even when there's no money in your pocket – not even a dime.
We will survive because money isn't everything.
Ask any reader of God's word how thirty pieces of silver did Judas in.
We will survive because Jesus really cares.
He showed us all how to love – with your burdens, cast all of your cares.
We will survive lets me know
That the problem could be bigger – you just have to let go.

Let go and let God work it out for you.
For you will survive, and Jesus will see us through.

Give Us Strength

Lord, give us strength to carry on.
    Let us walk in victory and sing a new song.
A song of power – a song of praise
    to let the world know we need to be saved.
When the devils of Hell start to attack,
    the strength of Jesus will set satan back.
God give us strength to get us through
    the troublesome things in life which gives us the blues.
Give us the strength to give God a shout
    when everything seems to be out of control and we really start to doubt.
Give us strength according to your promise as you gave David, Israel's King.
    Give us strength from day to day
it makes us hope for a better day.
    Give us strength because you're strong.
We need your strength to carry on.

God the Creator

No matter how things are or what it seems to be,
have faith in God – the creator of you and the creator of me.
If God were to show you all the things that are ahead
knowing how you handle things, you would think you're better off dead.
This is why God has given us Jesus to show us how to live.
God loved his creation so much, His Son's life he did give.
In knowing this you should know that Jesus Christ is in control
But you say I can't see him – I don't know how.
You have a brain to think with and it can't be seen, but you know it is there.
You have a heart to share love – you can't see it, but you continue to live.

I believe in the invisible King Eternal who rose from the dead to free us from sin
to make a show of the devil that we would conquer sin.

Shout

Shout unto God with a voice of triumph – let the praises of our lips sing.
 O' what a joy this sound is sending – sending to our risen King.
Shout because you have the victory.
 Shout because the horse and rider were thrown into the Red Sea.
Shout with all your heart, your soul and your mind.
 This joyful noise is heavenly and divine.
Shout unto God, he will bring you out.
 Jesus is always listening if you have any doubts.
Shout for your loved ones so they can see
 that the shout is pleasing to God and it gives us the victory.

A Christmas Gift

Christmas day will be a day of joy for some.
Others have some pain – they have suffered the loss of a loved one.
But Jesus remains the same – let Jesus fill your heart with Christmas joy.
The little ones won't understand, they just want their toys.
Take the time to tell them about Jesus, the greatest gift to us all.
Tell them how God gave us life through Him that we might not fall.
Snowmen, reindeer, and Santa are not the reason why.
I believe it grieves the Holy Spirit when we start to deny
that Jesus is the reason for the season.
We are to train our children in the way that they should go.
Tell them how Christ came to us to save us from our sins.
To bring salvation to the world – for every man, woman, boy and girl.

With Thanksgiving

All the time we are blessed, God has given us his very best.
God is good all the time – even when the hills are hard to climb.
The mountains look steep and the rivers run deep.
The valleys are low and the strong winds may blow,
but with Thanksgiving I'll spiritually grow.
Jesus, I love you dearly and you need to know
I trust that you can take my sins and wash them white as snow.
With thanksgiving you will always be my strong tower to set my soul free.
Thanksgiving is not just turkey, trimmings and something to eat.
With thanksgiving is the love of Jesus, and that's a real treat.

Our Daily Bread

Thank you, Lord, for our daily bread.
Not only physically, but with thanksgiving we are spiritually fed.
Jesus, you are the Bread of Life.
With your wisdom and knowledge you put satan to flight.
It's the Living Word that gives us strength.
We thank God above for the gift that was sent.
Manna has fallen from the sky
and those testers who ate it surely died.
But when we eat of your flesh we shall never die.
Bread of Life how faithful and true.
The Word of God has come down from Heaven
to lead us to the other side of 'through.'
Our daily bread means I will never die
as long as I know that Jesus is still alive.

The Church

The church is supposed to be a place of worship for you and for me.
A place of refuge for those in need.
The church is not just a building or a museum so others can see.
The church is the holy ground of God to do His good pleasure also in thee.
Sometimes the church seems like it has lost the true identity
of what its purpose is on earth – to set the captives free.
We think it's just a social place to meet once a week
when God is looking down on us saying, "why are my people so weak?"
Gossip, murmuring, backbiting, and lies.
We as the church of Christ need to repent, understand our purpose and the reason why.
Why so many people stay away from the church.
And how others like to come just to gossip and get the 411 dirt.

When the church hurts you, where else is there to go?
  Then satan will come with empathy, setting you up for the fall.
He will try anything to make you feel at home.
  He knows how you feel – he wants your soul.
Church, let's get together in love and unity.
  Let's stand on God's Word and the church will be a better place to be.

The Son Will Shine

The Son came down to shine, but you would not understand.
Let me try to help you in knowing God's plan.
When most people think about the sun, they think about a ball of fire suspended in the sky.
The Son I want to tell you about didn't come to set, but on the third day arise.
Through the suffering and pain he endured the shame to give us the victory.
To let our light shine for all men to see.
How does it feel on a rainy, cloudy day?
The sun that you depend on can't save you or prepare you for the light of the way.
If you don't know who the light is, listen to these words I say.
Jesus is the way, the truth and the light.
His love is faithful, true and right.
Some people worship the sun – they lay prostrate in a slain position trying to change,
but deep down inside, they still remain the same.

The Son I want to tell you about – when you lay out prostrate and slain,
I guarantee you won't remain the same.
Jesus is our light on a cloudy day – give him a chance.
Let the light of the true Son shine within.
No matter what the sun is doing, let not these words be a surprise
because the Son of God will always shine.

Be Strong

Be strong, brother – be strong.
Be strong, sister – be strong.
My brothers and sisters, hold on to the Faith.
If you think living this Christian life is easy don't be fooled.
It takes a humbled heart and a Christ-like attitude.
The world thinks we are weak, but Christ says in Him we are strong.
Be strong my sister – be strong.
When you have been our support from the beginning of time,
let's unite our strength and blow satan's mind.
He doesn't want us to get along.
The devil knows when we get together on one accord,
that the love of Jesus will show up and teach us the way.
Hold on – hold on, I know it seems long
but my God is faithful, trouble won't continue to prolong.
We need each other – how true the matter tends to be.

The fact of the matter is, when I look at you, do you see Jesus in me?
Don't tear the brother down, lift him up; pray for him – fill his cup.
Brothers love your sister in a special way for she is really tender in her ways.
This was God's way – he made her by his design.
This is ordained by God – true and divine.

When Trouble Arises

Lord, who shall I call on when trouble arises?
My heart often wonders, "Does He hear me when I cry?"
Why does He make me wait in hard times like these?
There is nothing else to be said or done.
Just hold to His hand and trust in Him, please!
In all of your waiting, I am that I am is creating.
Making you into His mold to let you know that He is the one who is in control.
Keep on doing what is right.
Keep Jesus on your mind and give the devil a good fight.
God watches over us all in times like these
to pour us out a blessing to meet our every need.

Thy Name is Lord

O' Lord, thy name is everything to me.
What is there on the earth that You have not sustained?
Your sun gives me warmth; your moon lightens the darkness of my nights.
Your grass comforts me when I fall; your waters give me life.
Your winds let me know that I can feel your presence.
Your snow reminds me of how pure, clean and true you are.
Without You, O' Lord, what can I do?
To know You is love, but Your wrath is unbearable.
My burdens are at times too heavy, but your mercies are new every morning.
Great is Thy faithfulness.
Your stars tell me that You are not far from me.
Your son Jesus is a part of me.
To all other little gods Your power is greater and divine.
For You, O' Lord, are one of a kind.

Each day I need You, and when I pray I thank You all the time.

Thou Has Walked With Me

O' Lord, my King, You are forever present.
When my enemies came upon me to trap me, You made a way of escape for me.
Thou art a God of love for His people in whom ye created.
The One You sent has never failed,
for I also trust that You created Him in the beauty of holiness.
You gave Him a name above every name – King Jesus.
Thou has walked the earth with compassion.
Thou has walked the earth with truth.
Thou has walked the earth with love.
Thou has walked the earth with peace.
Thou has walked the earth with power.
Thou has walked the earth with praise.
Thou has walked the earth with authority.
Thou has walked the earth with integrity.
Thou has walked the earth with sadness.
Thou has walked the earth with victory.
Thou has walked the earth with joy.
Thou has walked the earth with disciples.
But most of all – Thou walks the earth with me.

Think of the Eternal

Eternal is God, it lasts forever – never fading or abating.

Eternal is hope to cast all your cares.
A hope for your future to make you aware.

Eternal is God's grace to give you faith,
to strengthen you in this Christian race.

Eternal is love to show you that He is there,
surrounding you with loved ones who will always be there.

Eternal is your God – the beginning and the end.
Make Him your eternal and cling to Him.

Eternal is Jesus, He lived to die.
Save our souls – eternally alive!

There is a God

People often say that there is no God.
As a believer in Christ, I find that statement to be awfully wrong.
I ask the unbelievers the reasons why.
We have on earth such beautiful oceans, seas and skies.
Fish, birds, trees and mountains that peak to the highest of highs.
Lands that are rich with oil to give us heat and supplies.
Flowers with a sweet fragrance, a scent from up above.
I thank Him for His spirit that descended on Him that day like a dove.
Why is the sun able to rise?
It is the power of God, don't act as though you are surprised.
God gives us the power and the strength to be alive.
It rains on the unjust, as well as you and me.
There is a God and it's plain to see he has given us gifts to share with those who don't believe.

The Provider

Jehovah Jireh, my provider.
Your grace is sufficient for me.
My wants are not a factor, but for my needs I depend on thee.
My vow I must pay, for your blessings are great.
One tenth is all that you require.
To pay it is my heart's desire.
My first fruits I give you and thy benefits.
I love to see food on my people's table.
My joy is great for supplying this need with outstretched arms.
O' Lord, Jesus paid his tithe – it was more than a tenth.
God gave his son to die.
God, you never forsook me, you heard my humble cry.
And since that day I started giving the tenth I've never lacked in supply.

<u>The King</u>

Where shall I go that you have not been?
What shall I see that your hands haven't created?
Why should I fear for your love is fearless.
When will I see the wicked in defeat?
How shall my mind attain it?
Victory is yours for this I know,
Jesus is the hope of tomorrow.
Saints, do ye yet not know?
I ask these questions for you to know why.
How He hung on Calvary's cross for you and I.
With a little doubt in the garden He could have said no.
But with no fear, He prayed to the Father and said, "I will go."
Father you created so much for them to see.
I've come to give strength on earth – love, power and unity.
I've come to destroy the works of satan.
Also to give hope to a chosen nation.

For out of Israel one shall arise
to reign as King forever – Christ the most high.

Thank You, Lord

Thank you, Lord, for the good times you have shared.
With your love you showed me the way when no one else was there.
Thank you for allowing me to see how much you care.
You are a true friend indeed – you handled all the things I could not bear.
Thank you, Lord, for helping me in troubled times.
When satan buffets, I know this battle is not mine.
Thank you, Lord, for Jesus who took on the task
of saving those who believe from the devil's attack.
Thank you, Lord, for all my basic needs –
food, shelter, clothes and health – without them, where would I be?
Thank you, Lord, for an example like Saul;
transforming him into a great preacher by the renowned nature of Paul.

Thanking you, Lord, does not seem to be enough.

Thank you anyway-You are always there when the going gets tough.

The Peace of God

Peace is the part of God that we seem to lose
when the trials of this life get the best of you.
Patience will always bring you to know
that enduring these challenges will help you to spiritually grow.
Like a tree planted by the rivers, ye shall not be moved.
Every test that you have in life has to be approved.
The devil just can't come in and wreak havoc in our lives.
He has to have permission from God, which cuts him like a knife.
The devil lost his privileges a long time ago.
Saints of God, he still thinks he is the one in control.
Don't let that liar steal your peace or your joy – praise and shout!
The fact of the matter is Jesus will bring you out.

Now that you have heard, let the Peace of God and His word always have the final say
They will let you live peacefully in the trials of life today.

A New Day

Our new day has begun.
  Our yesterdays were fun.
Our tomorrow God holds.
  Our faith in the future He will mold.
Each day is unexpected – it's something to behold.
  You are a miracle, haven't you been told?
His grace is always present, it never fades away.
  Regard the day in Him – He'll show you the way.
When you awake in the morning give God the praise.
  For his sweet Holy Spirit allowed you another day.

Never Alone

We serve a God who really does care.
In times of trouble He is always there.
Sometimes we think we are all alone –
looking for hope or for someone to phone.
But the line is busy – it never fails;
you're trying to call on someone who can't help in times of despair.
Friends are always good to share secrets, joyous times and cares.
When the time comes and you can't get through,
fall on your knees – call Jesus, he will be there for you.
He is not hard to find.
There is a familiar saying, "Jesus is on the main line."
Take the time to call him when no one else is there.
When others are too busy to listen, my God is always there.
Have patience in Him – he's a friend indeed.
With Him you are never alone.

He has brought you this far and He will give
you strength to go on.
You are never alone means that Jesus does care.
The Lamb of God, the great sacrifice, will
not put anything on you that you can't bear.
In your time of thinking have faith to bring you to the point of believing
you are never alone – Jesus is always there.

In the End

In the end I want to see all of God's children
shout the victory.
Because of the pain and suffering that you
caused,
our purpose in life was put on pause.
Our God had to stop and really think of a
way
to show us his love in a special way.
The conversation was three-fold:
God, Jesus and the Holy Ghost were in control.
The plan was simple, "Son you go to the
earth
and stop this rage with the power of Heaven
and the Holy Ghost."
Show my people that there is only one way
to stop the devil and his lies;
repent, repent, repent before you die.
In the end my bible tells me because of
deception, lies and false doctrine you'll see
the lake of fire as your destiny.
Then the children of God will stand tall with
a shout.

In the end God's way is the truth – and that's no doubt.

Lift up Thy Holy Hands

My God, my God I trust in thee – the only help that I know.
Who shall be the one to save me? – tis Jesus, yes I know.
In prayer I see Peter with His arms extended high,
not keeping his mind stayed on Jesus, Peter thought he was about to die.
But my God is faithful, the one who never lies
extended his mighty hand and said hold to the truth and arise.
Worship the Lord in spirit and truth
for you'll see His great glory and His benefit too!
Moses had to stand on a rock just to see –
with extended arms the Egyptians did flee.
So lift up your hands and give God the praise.
Remember Peter and Moses and how salvation came unto them in a special way.

Birthday Wish

When you came into this world some were saying boy and some were saying girl.

It really did not matter to me – you will always be my precious sunbeam.

I've seen the cutest little baby things and it gives me great joy to see the happiness it brings you!

The toys or the shoes or the books or the clothes will never compare to the love Mimi has for you, Ellis.

I will always be there.

Every year about this time, we hope that in the future each birthday will be one of a kind.

My precious, Ellis, you are growing wonderfully!

God is truly blessing you now with many abilities.

With love all around you in many different ways, honor your father and mother.

By doing so God promises that you will have longer days on this earth.

Don't forget to honor MiMi – remember, I was your Mommie's Mom's first.

This birthday will be special – always know that your family comes first.

Stay connected and be directed. While growing into a Man, you will look back and see

what a joy that it will be for you and all your birthdays will be fond memories!!!

I love you my precious, Ellis.

Your MiMi

Goodness and Mercy

Goodness and Mercy, you have followed me.
Two never-ending friends who kept me from dangers seen and unseen.
It is Goodness that helps us get through the day
and shows us His love in the world today.
Mercy, Mercy is our cry when tragedies are about to arise.
We call on you faithfully, thinking that we are going to die.
You are also spirits that we tend to forget
and your faithfulness in following us has never failed us yet.
Goodness, you are excellent in character and in state.
You complement Mercy so well that King David called on you in his time of fate.
Just like you followed David, please follow me.
I will call on you more faithfully – not only in times of need.
Two spirits that work so well in harmony.
The two dwell as one, protecting us daily.

Thank you Goodness and Mercy for not just following King David in his trials and tragedies;
you also were gracious enough to follow me.

Death Has Been Defeated

When death comes our way it's hard to understand why.
When death comes our way we must all say our good-byes.
When death comes our way it's time to draw nigh
to the one who defeated death – our Lord who reigns on high.
It's just a form of sleep eternal – the soul is still alive.
The spirit of Jesus is calling you, waiting for His precious children to arrive.
Death is a part of life, something we can't escape.
So all you parents with little ones, teach them that Jesus is the gate.
A gateway to Heaven where all the saints will go
to live with Him forever in a resting place, this I do know.

So families, pastors, preachers and friends, let's teach them the reason why
death has been defeated and the grave is still denied.
Jesus lives forever – so will you and I.

Angels

Hark, the Herald Angels sing, glory to the newborn King.

Let us take the Angels' example and lift our voices and sing.

Exalting God with the highest praise!

Hallelujah! Hallelujah! Thank God I'm saved!

Angels were created to minister in a special way.

Look in your Bible and see how the Angels came to Jesus when the tempter saw that he was hungry.

He tempted Him for forty days and let's not forget the forty nights!

God also provided the Angels with an anointed light.

Angels are everywhere, they come in different shapes, colors and sizes.

Therefore, the next time that you encounter a beggar, think before you react.

It could be an Angel in disguise.

Be careful how you treat others – show love, kindness and compassion.
That beggar could very well be your Angel (unaware).
Thank you, Lord, for Michael – a warrior in the sky.
He helped kick out satan when his carnal mind started to rise.
Gabriel, your presence is also to be known.
You deliver messages that come directly from the Throne.
Angels are worthy, but not to be praised.
Angels worshipped Jesus as He endured the Cross for you and me that day!

Cathy's Prayer

O' Lord, I know that you see me each and every day.
The devil is also looking and trying to pull me into His ways.
It is always a fight because satan does not want me to do right.
And in Jesus' name I will continue to remain–
doing whatever it takes to dwell in Heaven's gates.
My work is not finished and it is never ever too late.
I will just keep on doing what I am doing and keep the faith.
God knows that it is not easy – He said, "it would not be."
He said, "not to worry – I have overcome the world you see."
Your joy is not in that bottle that you use for your job each day.
Your joy is in Jesus, and it is here to stay!!

Pastors

A gift from God, given with purpose to fulfill a charge.
The charge that was said on that special day- a hope for the congregation that Jesus sent him their way.
God, give our pastors strength, the power and soundness of mind
to work in the gifts of the spirit that is so divine.
God, in the same way you gave us Jesus – a leader in every way,
touch the hearts of our pastors to follow Christ's example of how he lived life each day!
I know that we are just human and sometimes fall short,
but our God has blessed us with Jesus to give us support.
Pastors, just remember that your leader is Christ and you are never alone.
You must listen to His voice – even lost sheep that went astray will return home.
For whatever reason or cause, like the Prodigal Son, open your arms wide,

receive them back with the love of Jesus – patient, long suffering and kind.

I thank God for our Pastors who preach the word
and humble themselves so that others also can be heard.

A leader who follows Christ in word and deed
is a great pastor and God will be well pleased!

Peggy When You Sing

Peggy, when you sing the presence of God is ushered in.
The power of the Holy Spirit also resides within.
Your worship to God is one of a kind.
Your gift of singing is heavenly and divine.
Your singing is what makes the devil mad.
The fact of the matter is you have the job he once had.
Leading the worship that's what he used to do.
Now, Peggy, God has left it up to you.
Peggy, you are now being blessed, singing and setting the captives free.
Preparing the way for preachers to proclaim the victory.
Keep on singing with fervor and the power of God.
Pay no attention to anyone's face –
just look to our Jesus, the author and finisher of your faith.
If they only knew what God has done for you

then they would stand in agreement and worship God, just like you.

Suffering for Jesus

Lord, each day I see the Christians struggle and cry.
Sometimes tears of pain, only you, Lord, know why.
But, my God, this suffering is only to decide
do I want to follow Jesus or simply give up and die?
When I study about your suffering and how you had to bear the cross
it makes me feel that my sufferings are nothing – you paid it at no cost.
Your life you gave freely – what a debt to pay.
You had a chance to decline, but you saw that our suffering could not be denied.
Your sufferings were great and it was our prize.
So all these things that we go through as Christians and wonder why,
just remember this about Jesus – how he suffered – where, when and why.

Time

Before lands, tree, oceans, seas, rivers, birds, bees –
I could go on and on you see – I was in time and time was in me.
In my time I'm never too late.
My time is your time so, beloved, just learn patience and wait.
You rush through the day keeping a steady pace,
worried about the tick-tock of the clock as though you won't finish the race.
The race is not given to the swift nor the strong.
This race isn't about quickness or strength because time will go on.
There are days when we think time is really flying because of the activities of a fun filled day;
when in fact time remains the same.
It all boils down to this point – when you focus on the clock
your mind tends to stop concentrating on the time.

This is a concern of mine.
You should try to enjoy each and every day.
The Master of time has given us a new day.
Time is God – the beginning and the end.
Time is short for satan – the book of Revelation states this in the end.
Therefore, the next time you're asked for the time of day,
give it to them gladly because you know that God is the way.
Remember that time is God and God is time and that the clock is just something to see.
The real time is in Jesus and He has time enough for you and for me.

Wake Up, Wake Up

Wake up, wake up – stop living this lie.
Thinking you're cool and you're about to die.
Living a life that's gonna catch you with a surprise.
Wake up, wake up before you're the next one to die.
Those who die in Christ don't die in vain.
Our souls go to Heaven with Jesus, where we will remain.
To the believers in Jesus we are not afraid to die.
We know that our Father is the Most High.
So think about your life and the reason why God brought you all here today-listen to His cry.
There is more to life than trying to be cool,
partying all night and just acting like a fool.
Give your life to Jesus, He'll fix it now.
Wake up, wake up – He is in your town.
Be transformed in your thinking and don't spend your whole life drinking.

Wake up, wake up and arise before you get the devil's next surprise.
Satan wants to kill us anyway he can.
Get your house in order and let Jesus in.
Give Jesus your life, He will restore it back again.
It's never too late – forgiveness is his thing.
He will start you over with another chance.
Giving you new life, something that will last.

Mary, Mary

Mothers, thank you for your love and your care.
Thank you for your wisdom and the fruit that you bear.
Mary, Mary, mother of all – felt troubled in her heart by God's great call.
For the Angel had told her of this one thing, you shall bring forth a son named Jesus and he shall be King.
Only a woman could fulfill this task.
Only a mother could bring this to pass.
Mothers stay sweet, not just on this day – but always.
Elder mothers in the church, teach the younger mothers the way.
Show them how to be a mom, glorious and divine.
God has given you the experience, please share some of your time.
Some have lost their mothers and I can't say I really know how they feel.
However, Jesus is a mother to the motherless – He will help you through this ordeal.

Finally, I would like to say to all the mothers, no matter what your age,
God is blessing you every day and you have the greatest call –
Bringing new life into the world – what a blessing, what a charge.

ABOUT THE AUTHOR

Minister Donald Coad, a native of Baltimore, Maryland, is the youngest of three sons born to Hilda V. Coad and the late James Coad, Sr. His parents and brothers, James Coad, Jr. and the late David O. Coad, whom he greatly misses, have been some of the most significant influences in his life.

Donald has been preaching God's Word since 1994, seeking to walk as an example of God's property. He is a member of the Shiloh Church of Edgemere where he serves on the Men's Prison Outreach Ministry, visiting and sharing God's truth and encouragement to inmates at the Baltimore Corrections Facility.

Married since 1989 to lovely Antoinette, he is the father of three beautiful children, Donnisha, Brittany, and Joshua. He currently works as an Instructional Assistant at the Battle Monument School in Baltimore County, helping to teach and give dignity to severely and profoundly disabled youth. HE enjoys watching basketball, baseball, and football—

especially Baltimore's World Championship team.

This book has grown out of Minister Donald Coad's earnest desire to encourage everyone he meets with the truth of Jesus Christ. Little becomes much in the hands of the Lord.

www.ingramcontent.com/pod-product-compliance
Ingram Content Group UK Ltd.
Pitfield, Milton Keynes, MK11 3LW, UK
UKHW040017200726
13854UKWH00001B/248

9 780759 650053